ABOVE: Title Page from a 1660 printed copy of the Icelandic
Prose Edda, originally written by Snorri Sturluson in 1223.

This US edition © Wooden Books Ltd 2025
Published by Wooden Books LLC,
San Rafael, California.
www.woodenbooks.com

First published in the UK in 2023
by Wooden Books Ltd, Glastonbury, UK

Library of Congress Cataloging-in-Publication Data
Johnson-Bell, L.
North European Paganism

Library of Congress Cataloging-in-Publication
Data has been applied for

ISBN-10: 1-952178-45-2
ISBN-13: 978-1-952178-45-0

Designed and typeset in Glastonbury, UK
Printed in India on FSC® certified papers by
Quarterfold Printabilities Pvt. Ltd.

NORTH EUROPEAN
PAGANISM

Linda Johnson-Bell

The single-most life-enhancing aspect of my life, in all planes, is the study and practice of my Sámi and Finnish (Karelian) ancestor's view of the world. To them, I owe an enormous debt of gratitude.

"The sunrise every morning is all the miracle I need."
- my father, Helsinki 2019.

SOURCES: Oral traditions are notoriously hard to preserve in writing. Tacitus wrote Germania around 98 CE, mentioning encounters with Celtic druids, Sámi skiers, Germanic hoards, and magic Finns, but he may have copied lost texts from Pliny the Elder and others, and based his accounts on interviews with soldiers and traders. In Iceland we have Snorri Sturluson's Prose Edda (1222) and the Icelandic Codex Regius containing the Poetic Edda (1270). The Finns have the Kalevela (1835), the Balts the Kalevipoeg (1270), the Slavs the Primary Chronicle, compiled in Kyiv around 1111, and the Novgorod First Chronicle compiled in the Novgorod Republic in 1841. An unmissable read is Johannes Scheffer's The History of Lapland (1674).

Historical sources should be handled with care; they often reflect the perspectives and prejudices of their authors. Christian and nationalist sentiments inevitably colour many written and visual depictions of the peoples and cultures featured in this book.

ABOVE: Sámi shaman in animal clothing, in Sámi village. From Noord en Oost Tartaryen (North and East Tartaryen) by Nicolaes Witsen (1641-1717), Amsterdam 1705.

CONTENTS

ABOVE: *Bear hunt ritual. Mountain landscape of Lapland with
inhabitants, From J. Scheffer's* True and worthy history of Lapland, *Amsterdam 1682, engraved by Jan Luyken.*

INTRODUCTION

WE WERE ALL PAGANS, once. Animism was our first belief system. Wishing to make sense of both the physical and non-physical worlds, we imbued creatures, objects and places with spiritual essences. We gave them special significance and named them. We worshipped the forces of nature, we personified and then we named them too, modeling them after ourselves and the people in our tribes. Our power of language allowed us to tell stories about them, to create fictions. Thus, the Gods and Goddesses were born.

Our first religion, today relegated to the category of "indigenous belief" or "folklore", slowly threaded its way through time, migrating along with us in all directions. This means that in almost all polytheistic pagan traditions we are left not with clear, distinct and organized pantheons, but rather a messy family tree: a lineage rooted in aliases, dysfunction, multiple personalities and local variations. We carried our father Sun, our mother Earth and a few crazy aunts and uncles with us wherever we went, and they answered us. No matter by what name we called, they came.

The pagan traditions of northern Europe reveal a uniquely vibrant brand of polytheism, one that is born of seemingly disparate nation-states, but is in fact united by a shared circumpolar influence. Historical records of these oral traditions are sparse (*see notes on p.iv*) and attempts to draw distinct lines between, say, the various Indo-European and Finno-Ugric pagan traditions, as we do today with their geography, politics, and languages, are fraught with difficulties. Nevertheless, their extraordinary traditions continue to bind them to each other and attach them to the umbilicus of humanity.

THE NORTH EUROPEAN PAGANS
a motley crew

The potpourri of Indo-European & Finno-Ugric nations, across what we now call northern Europe, share a long history of a united pagan faith with shamanism as the strongest common denominator.

What differentiates North European paganism from its classical Greek and Roman cousins is its close ties to nature, and an honoring of the gods, as opposed to an appeasement. The North European pagans viewed their gods and goddesses as friends and family, as allies with whom they had personal relationships.

The enduring appeal of Northern European paganism is perhaps less about the way it coped with Christian colonialism than the way it learnt to survive alongside it, in the guise of a thriving folklore.

ABOVE: The Northern European groups of this book: The SÁMI (Lapland), FINNIC (Finland), BALTIC (Estonia, Latvia & Lithuania), NORDIC (Denmark, Norway, Sweden, Iceland, Greenland & Faroe Isalnds) and SLAVIC (Russia, Ukraine, Poland, Czechia, Slovakia & Slovenia). They travelled extensively; an ancient Icelander would likely have had more in common with an ancient Estonian than their counterparts today. OPPOSITE: Traditional fishing house, Reykjavik, Iceland, 1835.

3

ANIMISM
spirits in everything

Our ancestors were ANIMISTS (from *anima*, 'soul' or 'spirit' in Latin). They believed that all things, even words, were imbued with spirit, either intrinsically, or because they were inhabited. This enabled humans to communicate directly with animals, plants, rocks, rivers, mountains, and even inanimate objects like tools and artifacts. Prehistoric religion saw humans as another part of nature, and animism was born from that relationship. The personification of inanimate objects, plants, and natural phenomena was the first spark of the notion of a soul, and an understanding that there was a power beyond, though not necessarily above them. The belief in a spiritual world outside the body evolved into a belief in an afterlife, with rituals around the burial of the dead with special objects.

Animism manifested in the worship of spirit animals—totem objects, river gods, sacred places, holy springs, guardian spirits, amulets and animal cults—and the need for an intermediary to travel between the worlds: a priest or shaman (*p.10*).

4

The Hazardous Mountains

The Violent Wind Circius

The Art of Prophecy

The Fury of Cyclones and Hurricanes

The Varying Shapes of Ice

Combat with Sirens of the Wood

Finns selling the wind

Women skilled in magic

SPIRIT ANIMALS
totems, talismans, amulets and cults

The Sámi have over one thousand words to describe the attributes of reindeer, their most important totem animal. For example, *rjebbe* is a calf with a huge belly, *lurvi* means long and shaggy fur, and *njirru* is an uncontrollable female! Reindeer antlers are symbolic of the world tree and were worn by shamans as a talisman to attract or embody the power and spirit of the animal (as opposed to amulets which ward off negative energy, evil or illness). Hunting societies treated the animals they killed for food with respect, so others of their species would not 'refuse' to be caught, and honored what the animal provided for the community. So intense was this spiritual kinship that some Sámi tribes believed that they were descended from the reindeer or bear.

Northern European paganism is full of the creature companions of shamans and witches—cats, ravens, bears, pigs, wolves, doves and horses—and tended to match their character. These are FYLGJUR. The fylgja's fate is tied to that of its owner. Odin had his two wolves, two ravens, and grey horse. OSTARA, the Goddess of Spring, had two hares. SKADI, the Goddess of Winter, had an arctic fox. The Slavs were worshippers of horse and bear (*see bear cults, see p.20*).

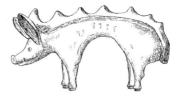

6

ABOVE: Wolves in the snow, John Savio,
c.1930. Wolves were key spirit animals.

LEFT: Sámi hunter on skis, with animal
assistant. The Sámi people invented skis.

FACING PAGE: Bronze wild boar. Rock
art, 4000–1000BC, Alta, Norway.

BELOW: Sámi shaman in a trance, with
conjured magical animals. His wife stands
guard above him. Olaus Magnus, 1555.

WATER WORSHIP
springs, rivers and saunas

The Slavic creation story opens: "At first, there was nothing but water". So, of all the elements, water may be the most sacred. Many temples and shrines were built near water. Wells, springs, streams, oceans and lakes have been central to almost all pagan shamanic rituals of cleansing, healing and birthing.

The word "sauna" is thought to derive from the Uralic SAVŃA, a heated pit covered with an animal hide, and some form of the sauna has been used by the Sámi and Finnish since at least 7,000BC. The Balts constructed holy bathhouses for rituals from birth to funereal rites. The Vikings allegedly used wells as sites for human sacrifice.

Such is the liminal appeal and power of water, it has spawned deities in every pantheon since the dawn of time. For the Slavs, Sámi, and Finns, rivers and springs were thresholds between the realms of the living and the dead, the dwelling place of the RUSALKI, the souls of those who died unnatural deaths.

However, with Christianisation, came the banning of water worship (and tree veneration too), as early as 452. In 960, the Saxon King Edgar required every priest to "extinguish heathenism and forbid the worship of fountains".

ABOVE: *Skjeggedalsfos, Hardanger, Norway.* RIGHT: *Odin gains wisdom from drinking at Mimir's well.* BELOW: *A Stalo.* OPPOSITE: *Aino hears the väki calling her into the water.*

SHAMANISM
communicating with the spirits

Across the world, the shaman acts as an intermediary between the human and spirit worlds, often with the aid of natural hallucinogenics combined with ritual, music and song. The shaman thus enters a trance, an altered state of consciousness, for their journey. The Siberian Tungus tribe's word *săman* means "one who is excited, moved, raised".

The shaman would ask the spirits for the time of the reindeer migration, or when to set sail. They were the doctor, lawyer, therapist, ombudsman, astrologer, weather forecaster, counsellor, priest and keeper of myths, stories and history. Upper Paleolithic cave paintings show evidence of shamanistic practices from at least 30,000 years ago.

Shamans were often female, with older women being guardians of the ancestors. One woman found in the 834AD Oseberg ship burial had a leather pouch filled with cannabis and henbane, and was likely a VÖLVA, a Norse seeress. The Slavs had female and male witches, VEDMA and YEDMAK (from the Proto-Slavic *vědět*, to know). The Finnish had NOITA and the Sámi NOAIDI. The Sámi Story of Myandash relates:

> *"His name was Myandash and his mother was a shaman and a Sámi witch who had the ability to transform herself as a reindeer."*

ABOVE: *A Sámi shaman playing a Lur horn.* RIGHT: *A Norse Völva, schooled in seidr (magic),*
offering community insight. BELOW: LEFT: *Sámi shaman from Trøndelag with his painted drum.*
RIGHT: *Another Sámi shaman, by Samuel Rheen, 1671.* FACING PAGE: *Details of Völva's staffs.*

THE SHAMAN'S SONG
the voice of nature

Repetitive rhythms have long been known to affect human brainwave activity and move participants into altered states of consciousness. From Siberian and Mongolian throat singing to the boisterous Viking drinking songs that were sung alongside poems and stories, live trance music is nothing new.

The Old Norse word for magic, GALDR, comes from their word *gala*, meaning "to sing, to charm, to enchant". Historians suspect their spells may have been chanted in a falsetto, sounding similar to their KULNING, an ancient YODEL

used as a herding call. There was also the VARDLÖKKER, the trance song of the völvas, the female shaman seeresses. The völva was sung to by maidens during her SEIDR (magic), sending her off to other worlds. The vardlökker was personal to each völva.

A JOIK, meanwhile, was an incantation which drew the singer closer to what they were thinking about. One does not joik *about* something, one joiks something's essence. So potent was this magic singing that it was banned until the 1988 Sámi Act.

ABOVE: A healing joik. Not all joiks contain words: in a sound, a person or place can be imagined. LEFT: Finnish and Karelian shamans used the kantele, a plucked string instrument, to draw themselves into their visions. Here Väinämöinen plays the kantele and Nature stops trembling to listen to the wonderful notes that soar from the magical instrument.

MAGICAL FORMS AND TOOLS
staves and runes

Magic is all about transformation. Churn milk into butter. Weave wool into a tunic. Brew hops into beer. Turn love into children. Raise children into adults. To change futures, minds, and more subtle forms of energy the Norse used crystals, meditated, read runes, threw bones, and participated in BLÓTS and ceremonies (the word "rune", from the Old Norse rúnir/ rúnar, means "magic signs, hidden lore").

GALDRABAKUR grimoires in Iceland reveal runic inscriptions, staves (*see examples opposite*) and symbols used in spell work, GALDRAMYNDIR. The Norse VÖLVA practiced TROLLDOM (magic spells), GALDR (chants and incantations), SEIDR (communication with spirits), SPÁ (or SPAE, divination and prophecy), and runic magic. Sámi NOAIDI practiced GAND with which they told fortunes, controlled the wind, found lost objects, and cast spells. Slavic 'white' witchcraft was centred on love spells and healing, often practised with ancient herblore by wise grandmother crones called BABA YAGAS. On their oval, reindeer-skinned frame drums, GOAVDDIS, Sámi shamans would draw symbols to form cosmological maps of the underworld (*see below, and pages 35–37*).

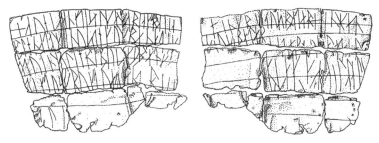

ABOVE: *Lead amulet from Lille Myregård on Bornholm. Drawing by Lisbeth M. Imer,*
National Museum of Denmark. FACING PAGE: LEFT: *A Sámi Noaidi playing a decorated*
reindeer-skin drum. CENTRE & RIGHT: *Sámi drum designs, Jan Luyken, 1682.*

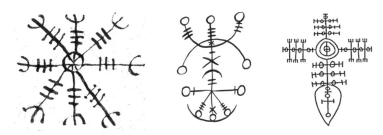

ABOVE: *Galdrastafir, Icelandic magical staves.* L to R: *Ægishjálmr (Helm of Terror),*
for protection of a warrior in battle; Nabrokarstafur (Dead Trousers) for endless wealth;
Sheildmaiden's Stave. From a famous early collection of Icelandic magical staves, sigils and
charms by Geir Vigfússyni á Akureyri in 1847. BELOW: *The runic futhark (alphabet).*

F	U	Th	A	R	K	G	W	H	N	I	J
FEHU	URUS	THURIZAS	ANSUZ	RAIDO	KANU	GEBO	WUNJO	HAGALL	NYEDIS	ICE	JERA
Own	Auroch	Thorn	Ash	Ride	Ulcer	Gift	Win	Hail	Need	Ice	Year
wealth	power	giant	mouth	road	fire	talent	joy	havoc	night	freeze	harvest

EY	P	Z	S	T	B	E	M	L	NG	D	O
EYWAS	PERTHO	AELGHIZ	SOWULI	TEIWAZ	BERKANAN	EHWAZ	MANNAZ	LAGU	INGWAZ	DAEGAZ	OTHALA
Yew	Pear?	Elk	Sun	Warrior	Birch	Horse	Man	Lake	Living	Day	Heritage
strength	game	defence	light	victory	birth	progress	intellect	lagoon	fertility	dawn	estate

WEAVING
the sacred threads of fate

Under the world tree **YGGDRASIL**, beside the *Urðarbrunnr*, the sacred white Well of Urðr, sat the three **NORNS**, representing the Past, Present, and Future, weaving the threads of fate and reading their runes. They were the most powerful figures in the Norse world. Destinies were written at birth and carved into the trunk of Yggdrasil. Only a person's individual life force or **HAMINGJA** could reshape it.

Weaving has a symbolic function in all pagan traditions and was often performed by goddesses of fate, destiny, or time. What better, more tactile metaphor for the blending and intertwining of the connections we make in life? Even today, we use the term, "social fabric", acknowledging this belief that we are all connected.

The Balts had the **DEIVĖS VALDYTOJOS**, Lithuanian goddesses who wove garments from human lives. The Slavic trio of fate deities **ROZHANITSY**, **NARECNITSY**, and **SUDZHENITSY** (*below*), held a spindle and wove golden threads.

Orkney Woven Hood

ABOVE: *Woollen Fabric, c.500BC, found in a bog with the Haraldskær Woman, Moss of Haraldskjær, Jutland, in 1835.*

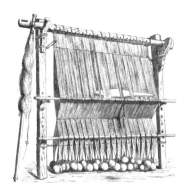

ABOVE: *12th century vertical loom from the Viking Faroe Islands, using stones as weights to keep tension.*

ABOVE: *The three Norns. Sisters, URDR (past), VERDANDI (present) and SKULD (future) wove the threads of life and carved their runic prophesies.*

ABOVE: *Woven forms also appear in Norse art. Carved runestone from Ryda, Uppsala, Sweden.*

WORLD TREES
bridges between worlds

All North European pagan traditions have a vast world tree as the central symbol in their respective mythologies.

In Norse mythology, there is YGGDRASIL (Old Norse *Mimameidr*), a gigantic ash tree that connects the nine worlds of Norse cosmology (*see below and opposite*). Yggdrasil has three roots, one in ASGARD (the home of the gods), one in JOTUNHEIM (the realm of the giants), and one in NIFLHEIM (the land of mist and darkness).

The Sámi's tree is a pillar (STYTTO) that reaches to the North Star and props up the universe, a bridge between the living and the dead.

The Baltic peoples share an oak/ linden tree which connects their three worlds: the upper world of the gods (KALNO KARIUOMENES), the human middle world, and the underworld of the dead.

The Latvian DABAS OZOLS "Tree of Nature" was an oak or birch. The Sun goddess SAULE hung her starry belt on its branches each night as she went to bed.

Finnish and Estonian runic songs tell of an oak tree with a bird at the top, stars entwined in its branches, and a snake slithering amongst its roots.

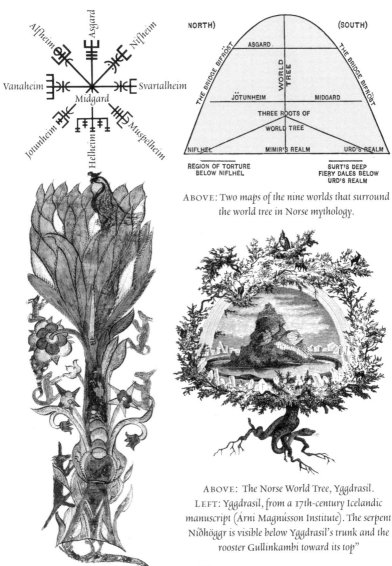

ASGARD
Álfheim — Asgard — Nifheim
Vanaheim — Svartalheim
Midgard
Jotunheim — Muspelheim
Helheim

<table>
<tr><td>NORTH)</td><td></td><td>(SOUTH)</td></tr>
</table>

THE BRIDGE BIFRÖST — ASGARD — THE BRIDGE BIFRÖST

WORLD TREE

JÖTUNHEIM — MIDGARD

THREE ROOTS OF

WORLD TREE

NIFLHEL — MIMIR'S REALM — URD'S REALM

REGION OF TORTURE
BELOW NIFLHEL

SURT'S DEEP
FIERY DALES BELOW
URD'S REALM

ABOVE: Two maps of the nine worlds that surround
the world tree in Norse mythology.

ABOVE: The Norse World Tree, Yggdrasil.
LEFT: Yggdrasil, from a 17th-century Icelandic
manuscript (Árni Magnússon Institute). The serpent
Níðhöggr is visible below Yggdrasil's trunk and the
rooster Gullinkambi toward its top"

19

BEAR CULTS
björnfesten and berserkers

"Wake up, my brother! The sun is already shining onto the forested hills!" So begins the Sámi bear hunt joik. As winters turns, hunters go to the frozen forest to look for hibernation dens. When one is found, the shaman is consulted before a hunter enters, awakens the bear, slays it, and drags it back to the SIIDA. The feast requires three days of preparation, beginning with an apology to the bear. The carcass is carefully buried to appease the bear's spirit, and its skin is shot with arrows by the hunter's wife. The wives spit elder bark juice (representing menstrual blood) at each other's faces for protection.

The discovery of Neanderthal bear skull shrines and cave art in the Swiss Alps indicates that circumpolar bear worship was widespread from early times. For the ancient Slavs, the god VELES took the form of the bear, their most worshipped animal. For the Sámi and the Finnish, the bear was taboo—it was even forbidden to say "bear", lest one overheard the plans being made for its hunt and came to pay a visit. During a ritual feast, the bear was the honored guest, its skull lifted high into a pine or fir tree to allow its spirit to soar to the heavens.

ABOVE: A bear hunt. Later, the bear's carcass is whipped with birch branches and it is buried with its bones in exact order. Its jaw is attached to the belt of its killer with a ring.

ABOVE: Norse Berserkers embodied the strength and power of the bear by wearing their skins into battle.

ABOVE: Bjarke orders Hialte to drink the blood of the bear to make him stronger. Olas Magnus (1555).

FACING PAGE: Björnfesten – Shamanic rituals of sacrifice, and feasting to ensure a successful hunt and appease the spirit of the animal.

POLYTHEISM
the evolution of the gods

As local spirits became less relevant to growing populations and larger communities, animism evolved. Local spirits became subsumed into more archetypal personalities which reflected people's growing perspective of the world. In many early societies, the personification of the natural world developed into the creation of deities, amplifying animistic relationships, turning the forces of nature into gods and goddesses, and putting man and his fate in their hands.

This belief in many gods (which does not exclude a supreme god) characterizes most religions (except the monotheistic Abrahamic religions), from the ancient pantheons of Sumer and Egypt to those of classical Greece and Rome. Northern Europe was no exception.

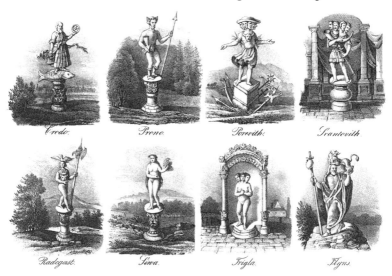

Credo.   Prono.   Porevith.   Svantevith.

Radegast.   Siwa.   Trigla.   Flyns.

ABOVE: The Sámi worship of a pagan Jubmel (general word for god), 17th C. engraving.
BELOW: The 14th C. Skog tapestry possibly depicting Norse gods Odin, Thor and Freyr.
FACING PAGE: Slavic deities, including: Radegast, Porevit and Svantevit.

GODS AND GODDESSES
friends and foes

North European pagan pantheons varied from highly organized to ramshackle, from national to local, and changed over time spans of 500 years and more. All had supreme gods and goddesses, and from them spawned often complicated and dysfunctional family trees. Their worship was often tied to the cycles of nature and to agriculture, and they were feted on the solstices and equinoxes. Some of them also had their own dedication days.

The Norse made their gods in their own likeness—passionate, ardent, and adventurous. They admired qualities like brutality, lust, humor, courage, strength, and guile. The best-known, **ODIN**, **THOR**, **LOKI**, and **BALDR** lived in **ASGARD**, a Nordic version of Mount Olympus. The Nordic tribes had a close, working relationship with their gods.

The Baltic gods too were intertwined within daily lives, but in a more pastoral or agricultural fashion.

The Slavic gods appear to have formed a more variable pantheon, with their worship more localized amongst specific tribes.

The revered pagan goddesses were honored with nurturing and fertile gifts. Their particular source of power was their connection between their fertility and that of the Earth.

In later pages we will meet many of these colorful characters.

ABOVE: The Finnish air goddess Ilmatar. Resting in the primordial waters, she gave birth to the land, sky, Moon, Sun, stars and first humans. Joseph Alanen [1885-1920].

LEFT: Sacrifices to (left to right): tienaren, Sohnen, Stoorjunckaren, Gumman, dottren (the servant, the Son, the Grand Prince, the Wife, the daughter). From a study by Samuel Rheen, 1671.

OPPOSITE: Thor's hammer, Mjölnir.

GOD HOUSES
shrines, temples, and altars

Rituals to worship the gods or honor the ancestors were usually held outside, in groves, woods, on islands, hills, by sacred waters, caves, or near unusual physical landmarks (*e.g. stone configurations, opposite*).

The Norse gods were worshipped at sacred places (VÉ), in a LUND (grove) or HAUGR (mound or barrow), or at a HÖRGR (stone altar), until the 6th century when they began to build God Houses with central towers (*opposite*). The Slavic leader Vladimir of Kiev built a temple dedicated to six of his favorite gods around 978 CE. The Baltic tribes, who had previously only worshipped in holy groves, or ALKA (Lithuania), also later built round wooden structures as temples.

Sacred places tended to be on hills or mountaintops, as did burial grounds. Human sacrifice seems to have been rare. The Sámi did not practice it, instead using "reindeer, dogs, cats, lambs and hens".

LEFT: The temple at Old Uppsala, devoted to the Gods of the Aesis cult. In 1555, Olaus Magnus wrote: "It shimmers with a golden lustre. From the golden roof hangs a golden chain which winds all around the building. To the right a spring in which a person will be drowned as a sacrifice." It mimics Christian churches to the south.

LEFT: Unusual stone configurations were significant. The Sámi called these places seiti, the Finns, seita.

FACING PAGE: Birch twigs are erected around the Thorens-bäleten (images of Thor) on the Offer Lafwan (the sacrificial bench). Documented in 1674 by Johannes Schefferus. Outdoor altars with wooden carvings of the gods were common as places of worship.

BELOW: The 7th century Stora Hammars stone, from Gotland, Sweden, depicts a man being sacrificed on an altar. Late Viking period.

27

FESTIVALS AND SABBATS
the wheel of the year

The pagan calendar was based upon the growing season, the 365-day cycle of the Sun. The Sámi began their calendar on the darkest day of the year, winter solstice, praying the Sun would return after its winter hibernation; the Norse celebrated their YULE around the same time. DISTING (DISABLÓT) was an early spring rite at the first new moon in February (the Slavic calendar also followed the lunar and tidal cycles).

OSTARA (the Slavic VELJA NOC) was the spring equinox feast. The Sámi used equinoxes to time reindeer migrations. In May, fertility celebrations coaxed new plantings to life. Summer solstice was celebrated as LITHASBLÓT by the Norse, JĀNI by the Balts, KUPALA by the Slavs, and JUHANNUS by the Finns. Autumn equinox heralded harvest festivals, such as the Norse Fallfest. Animals not expected to survive the autumn were eaten, excess meat was smoked or frozen. Many of these festivals (*see p.58*) involved blood sacrifices, such as the Norse BLÓTS.

Portable Sámi wooden calendars recorded important weeks in the year for reindeer, fishing and foraging (*below*).

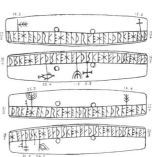

28

ABOVE: Dísablót was an ancient Norse festival held in honor of the female spirits known as dísir, with offerings of food, drink, and sacrifices made to them for protection and fertility.

Above: Old Norse Yule festival. Most pagan festivals were Christianised: the Spring Equinox became Easter; the Winter Solstice became Christmas, Harvest Festivals became Halloween.

ANCESTORS AND THE AFTERLIFE
adventures in the underworld

Like most ancient cultures, North European pagans believed in an afterlife. The Sámi believed that existence continued in a world called **SAIVO**, where game was abundant, full of relief from a harsh life. In the Slavic cosmology, the underworld was an eternal spring. If you were a Viking, you were greeted by the goddess **HEL**, with mead, good food, and a seat by the fire. The Baltic belief in reincarnation saw the souls of the deceased reincarnated in bird, animals, water, plants (especially trees). Objects were often placed with the dead (*e.g. the torc, below*).

The Finno-Ugric welcomed the spirits of their ancestors as helpful advisors in their daily lives. Finnish shamans were sent to **TUONELA**, the underworld, to seek knowledge or to bring back a **LUONTO** (guardian spirit) for the living. The Norse **ÁLFABLÓT** was a late autumn ancestral ritual where offerings in honor of an ancestor were made to elves who lived amongst the graves, by pouring animal blood over the burial mound.

Ancestor worship predates the emergence of gods. It engenders self-awareness—of the participant's important place in their lineage.

ABOVE: LEFT: Norse Valkyries, maidens who served the God Odin and guided souls of slain warriors from the battlefield to Valhalla, to live out eternity in drink and song. RIGHT: The Norse god Heimdal demands the return of the goddess Iðunn from the underworld.

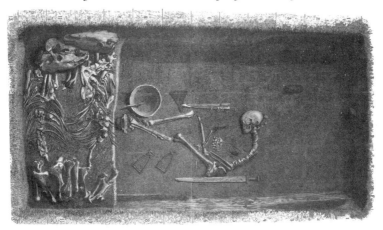

ABOVE: The Birka Warrior, a 10th century female Viking grave. She was buried dressed in a silk garment, with silver thread, along with two horses (a mare and a stallion), used weapons and armour, and a hnefatafl game set. FACING PAGE: LEFT: A 4th century torc (neck ring), Nousianinen, Finland. RIGHT: The Norse goddess Hel, ruler of the underworld, Hell.

THE SÁMI
shamans, snow and seidis

The Sámi are the indigenous Scandinavians, a semi-nomadic Finno-Ugric people who migrated from Siberia more than 3500 years ago. Originally inhabiting all of Fennoscandia, their diminished homeland is now an area named SÁPMI—a swathe of northern Norway, Sweden, Finland and the Kola Peninsula, (*see map below, c.1500*). Today there are about 70,000 Sámi left after centuries of persecution. In 1990, Norway recognized the Sámi as an indigenous people; they formed a parliament in 1993.

The Sámi are deeply animistic. They believe everything in nature has a soul, is alive and hallowed. Gods and goddesses (ATTJE) reflect natural features, such as rock formations (SEIDIS), springs, and natural forces. Their cosmos is composed of three tiers: the upper world of the ATTJE; the middle world of humans, animals and nature spirits; and SAIVO, the lower world and its god ROTAIMO, where the dead ancestors and spirit animals dwell. The dead sometimes dwelt at the bottom of the seemingly bottomless lakes of Sápmi, or in the sky as constellations. All tiers are housed under the fabric of the universe, woven into the branches of their tree of life, held up by the immutable and unmoveable North Star.

Their ancient shamanic animistic faith, set against the backdrop of their magical landscapes, meant that the Sámi were considered the most powerful wizards, diviners, and seers of northern Europe.

LEFT: The backdrop to the Sámi universe is one of icy nights, thick forests of fir and birch, northern lights and vast landscapes of quiet cold and whiteness, peppered with glacial erratics, the worshipped "seidi".

BELOW: Sámi life, 1735, showing their **LAVVU** houses, snow-shoes and baby sling.

SÁMI MYTHOLOGY
their gods and goddesses

The Sámi recognized many deities. MAHTARAHKKU was the mother Earth goddess. Her partner DIERPMIS, the thunder god, was depicted in wood with a nail in the head and a hammer (*see opposite*). BEAIVI was goddess (sometimes god) of the Sun, spring, fertility and sanity, symbolized by a cross in an oval (*opposite*); her daughter BIEJJENNIEJTE was goddess of medicine and healing. MÁNNO was goddess of the Moon, worshipped in silence at new moon. BIEGGAOLMMAI was god of winds and storms; with two shovels, he scooped the winds in and out of his cave. RADIEN was the sky god, symbolized by a pole; RAEDIEAHKKA was his wife, and RADIENPARDNE their son. LEABEOLBMAI, god of the hunt, dwelt among alder trees, occasionally appearing to humans as a bear. TJAETSIEÅLMAJ was god of lakes, rivers and fishing. ROHTTU was god of sickness and death, ruler of the land of the dead, ROTAIMO.

Along with the gods came giants, STÁLLU (stupid trolls, *e.g. below, by John Bauer*), DRAUGS (hosts of drowned people), ZARAHUS (sleep tormentors) and ČAHKALAKKIS (treasure guardians). All could be contacted by NOADI (shamans), to find out what needed to be done.

LEFT: Sámi people worshipping Horagalles. Picart, c.1730.

FACING PAGE: A Stállu. The Sámi also have a host of underground beings (GUFIHTARAT). In the north, they believe that their dead walk upside down in an inverted underworld, JABMEAIMO, "with the soles of their feet against those of the living on earth". The ULDA, invisible ancestor spirits, live in this inverted underworld in upside-down houses. They are rarely seen, but sometimes visit, especially if someone sets up their KOTA (house) directly above one of theirs; then an Ulda old woman will appear out of the woods and politely ask that the house be moved!

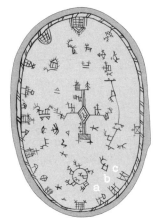

BEAIVI (SUN)

STORE HOUSE

ALTAR STONE

SACRIFICED ANIMAL

LEFT: Southern Sami drum, showing central cross motif of the Sun goddess BEAIVI. The three daughters of mother goddess MADER-AKKA also appear (bottom right): a: JUKS-AKKA, huntress, protector of children, who assigns fetuses their sexes. b: SAR-AKKA, goddess of fertility, menstruation, love, human sexuality, pregnancy and childbirth. c: JABME-AKKA, "akka of the dead", goddess of the mirror underworld.

35

A SÁMI DRUM
window into another age

The Sámi drum shown opposite was annotated by Olaus Stephani Graan in 1688. According to Graan, the central rhombus (1) represents the Sun; on the line to its left is Horagalles (2) with a thunder icon above him; to the right is Bieggolmai (3) with his shovels; above is a figure with a bow, hunting a female elk (4), possibly the huntress goddess Juksakka; below are three Ailekesolmak (5) who rule the holidays (holy days); the final low claw (6) shows where to place a small marker, whose bouncing passage was then interpreted, as the drum was played.

The left edge denotes the material world. Moving anticlockwise from the top, the top glyph is "the guardian spirit of the forest" (7, possibly Radien). Next, a "wild reindeer", then a figure for "clear weather" (8), then one holding two trees (9), the first labeled "snow" and the second "rain". Then a glyph representing "the forest where the elk and bear roam" (10), then "forest with squirrels" (11). Above this is "a beaver in its house" (12). There follows a storage house (13), and then a depiction of a Sámi camp with four (triangular) huts (14), followed by a glyph of a lake with two boats (15). At the bottom is a corral of reindeer (16).

The right side denotes the otherworld. Sarakka (17, fertility), is followed by Jabmeakka (18, harvest) and a "sorceress" shaman (19) with a spell overhead. Then, a corpse chest (20), another figure (21), an emblem of the moon/underworld (22), and Ruohtta (23, death). Along a line (24) we see a burial chest, then Ruohtta riding his horse, accompanied by two minions. Curving above (25) we find a goat, two god houses and two people. Two forest spirits close the circle (26). The upper interior figures are of a "boat" (27) and a "shadow boat" (28).

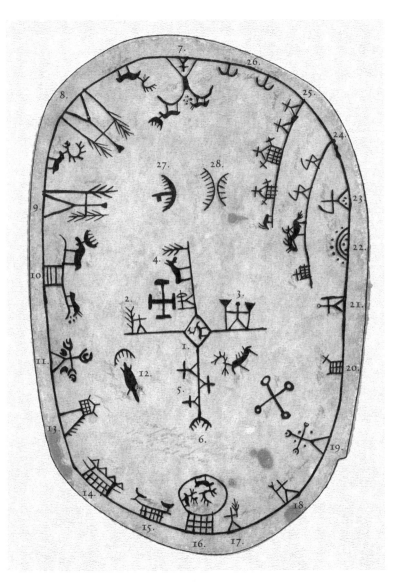

THE FINNIC TRADITION
and the Kalevala

The Finns (like the Sámi) have Uralic/Siberian circumpolar heritage. They were animistic, attending to ancestral spirits, guardian spirits and spirits of place, using NOITA (or TIETÄJÄ) shamans for guidance.

A key source of Finnish mythology is the *Kalevala*, an epic poem compiled in 1835 by Elias Lönnrot. The poem contains some cultural bias; for example, old pagan stories about the Finnish goddess LOVIATAR portray her as the goddess of the Moon. But as Finnish culture became more Christian, Loviatar was recast as LOUHI, goddess of the underworld, ruler of death and disease, an evil witch from the far north (a derogatory portrayal of female Sámi noaidi shamans).

In the *Kalevala*, Louhi and the POHJOLA (people of the underworld) fight the people of Kaleva and the shaman god VÄINÄMÖINEN, the book's hero. Louhi represents fading pagan beliefs, while Väinämöinen integrates the new faith, singing duels with his enemies and stealing back the SAMPO pillar, the Finnish world tree, from the underworld.

ABOVE: In the Old Kalevala an eagle lays its eggs on the knee of Väinämöinen. In 1849 Lönnrot published a New Kalevala in which a bird instead lays its eggs on the knee of Ilmatar (see p.25). "the Wind blew her womb full, the sea made her fat." The bird built its nest on her kneecap and laid its "six golden eggs and an iron egg the seventh". Ilmatar jerked her knee and the eggs burst into the dark space and the world was born.

LEFT: "Then arose three lovely maidens; ... mothers of the iron; ...bosoms overflowing with the milk of future iron." Painting by Joseph Alanen [1885-1920].

OPPOSITE: Louhi saves Väinämöinen. From the seventh song of the Kalevala.

39

Finnic Mythology
the spirits of nature

Finnish pagans worshipped local nature deities at shrines consisting of wooden statues or carvings of human figures in trees or tree stumps, or at **KUPPIKIVI**, "cup stones", large rocks into which small cups had been carved. They believed that everything in nature was imbued with a myriad of local spirits, known as **HALTIJAS** (sprites).

Haltijas could be found everywhere, in rocks, lakes, plants, animals and homes. Every being had its own **LUONTOHALTIJA** (nature spirit). Each person's soul, or **HALTIJASIELU** (soul sprite), consisted of three autonomous spirits: **HENKI** (or **LÖYLY**, life force, body), **ITSE** (spirit, soul, spark, self) and **LUONTO** (haltija, guardian spirit, character, animal power). When the henki left the body, the person would die, but the itse could travel outside the body, for example when dreaming, or in shamanic journeying, and the henki could reincarnate, life after life.

A **MAANHALTIJA** (land sprite) protected one's house and livestock, and was nourished by votive offerings at a shrine. These local haltijas were often the sacred spirits of venerated ancestors.

Haljitas were grouped into races of **VÄKI**, (throng), distinguished by their magical strength and qualities; e.g. there were väki of fire, water, forests, farmyards and graveyards. Väkis could become angry, so cursing close to a lake could make the water väki angry, causing illness and misfortune to befall you; while the fire väki is always angry; it always burns you, however respectful you are!

ABOVE: *Local natural animistic deities, Haltijass, could take human form. The Water Fairy, and The Fairy of the Snow, both by Ida Rentoul Outhwaite [1888 – 1960].*

ABOVE: *Lemminkäinen's mother, gathers the broken body of her son from the dark river of Tuonela, the Underworld realm of the dead. Painting by Akseli Gallen-Kallela, 1897.*

THE FINNIC PANTHEON
deities of sky, forest and water

AKKA (old lady), also known as RAUNI, was goddess of the Earth. Her daughter was MANUA, goddess of dry land. UKKO (old man) ruled the sky, and brought rain, swinging his hammer or shooting arrows to cause thunder; he was originally ILMA, god of the air (*opposite*).

MIELIKKI, or METSÄNEMÄ (mother of the forest), was the fierce goddess of forest, bears and hunting. She also brought luck, healing, beauty and abundance. Hunters would ask her permission before entering a forest. Her husband was TAPIO, god of the forest and its secrets (*below*). The old name for Finland was TAPIOLA.

The goddess of the sea and lakes was VELLAMO. Often shown as a mermaid, wearing a dress made of sea foam, she could control the wind and waves and grant fish to fishermen. Her husband was AHTI, god of the depths, giver of fish. Together they lived in the underwater palace of AHTOLA, along with various water spirits such as merman VETEHINEN and mermaid MERENNEITO.

PÄIVÄTÄR was goddess of the Sun, known for her silver jewelery and fine clothes. Her sister KUUTAR was goddess of the Moon. Together they controlled destiny as they wove the web of life. The original goddess of the moon was LOVIATAR, who later became LOUHI, the powerful goddess of shamanism.

LEFT: *The great smith* **ILMARINEN** *forged the dome of the sky and the* **SAMPO**, *mill of fortune. By Väinö Blomste, 1897.*

FACING PAGE: **TAPIO**, *husband of* **MIELIKKI**. *Their children were* **NYYRIKKI** *(god of hunting),* **TELLERVO** *(spirit goddess of the forest),* **TUULIKKI** *(spirit goddess of animals and the small wind),* **ANNIKKI** *(goddess of spinning) and* **KATAJATAR**, **PIHLAJATAR** *and* **TUOMETAR** *(spirit goddesses of trees).*

ABOVE: *The gods played a large part in traditional Finnish wedding ceremonies, blessing the luck of the happy couple. 1865 painting,* Wedding at Pohjola, *by Robert Wilhelm Ekman.*

43

THE BALTIC TRIBES
the last pagans in Europe

The Baltic pagans originated from Indo-Europeans who traveled to the area from the southeast during the Bronze age, fanning out in groups (*see map below*). Baltic paganism was chaotic, superstitious and tenacious—Latvia and Lithuania were the last European countries to convert to Christianity, although pagan traditions did survive and continue with the modern Romuva revival.

Baltic paganism is characterized by its use of fire in almost all rituals, even under sacred oaks in holy groves. The Lithuanian king Algirdas was known as a "fire worshiper" in the 1380s.

Sacred places, often groves of trees, known as **ALKAS** (or **ELKS**, "beautiful") were chosen for burnt sacrifices. In Latvia and Lithuania today, 120 hills or mounds (**ALKAKALNIS**), 70 fields (**ALKALAUKAS**), and 50 lakes (**ALKEŽERAS**), rivers (**ALKUPIAI**), islets (**ALKOSALOS**) and bogs (**ALKA OS**) still use the "alk" prefix.

Some Alkas remain in use, especially in the north of the region, where small groves of trees can still be found, surrounded by wooden chapels, crosses, and carved idols. A rich language of tapestry and decorative symbols also survives.

ABOVE: *Artists impression of the important Romuva sanctuary, described by Peter von Dusburg in 1326, with its priest, eternal sacred fire, evergreen oak and three idols.*

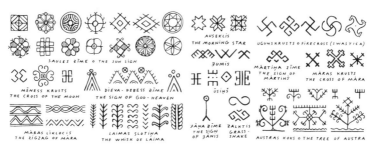

ABOVE: *North Baltic folk art symbols, and their associated meanings.* **MARA** *is the Latvian Mother Earth goddess, feminine counterpart to* **DIEVS** *(Dieva).* **LAIMA** *is goddess of Fate.*

45

BALTIC MYTHOLOGY
fire and fertility

The supreme Baltic sky god, charged with law and order, was DIEVAS. His counterpart was MARA (in some traditions ŽEMYNA or SAMYNA), goddess of earth, fertility and motherhood. Together with LAIMA, the goddess of destiny, they controlled the fate of humankind. Some traditions have Laima married to Dievas' powerful son PERKŪNAS, the god of thunder, lightning and fire. The underworld was ruled by the goddess RAGANA (or VELNS), or in some regions by another of Dievas' sons, VELINAS, the horned shapeshifting god of forest animals, assisted by his sister GILTINE, feared judge and protector of the natural order.

SAULĖ was the sun-goddess who crossed the sky every day in her chariot, bringing life, fertility and warmth. She was married to MĖNUO, the handsome god of the Moon, and their children were the stars, ŽVAIGŽDĖS, and the planets VAIVORA (Mercury), VAKARINĖ (Venus, evening star), ŽIEZDRĖ (Mars) and INDRAJA (Jupiter). However, Menuo fell in love with the morning star AUŠRINĖ, the goddess of dawn and beauty, so Perkūnas cut him in half, which is why he continues to wax and wane today.

MEDEINĖ (ŽVORŪNĖ) was the hare-like goddess of the forest, trees and animals. VĖJAS (VĖJOPATIS) was the unpredictable god of the winds and air, associated with storms and other natural phenomena, and master of Paradise (which was guarded by AUŠTARAS, cousin of Aušrinė). MILDA was the beautiful goddess of love and fertility.

GABIJA was the red-robed flame-haired goddess of fire, protector of the home and hearth—even today, salt and bread are left out for her.

RAGUTIS and his wife RAGUTIEN looked after guests and parties.

ABOVE: Early depictions of Baltic pagan Alkas or sacred groves with idols, altars and offerings, and a fire. The image on the left reads "Sacra quercus", or "Sacred oak".

ABOVE: Left to right: God of the underworld VELINAS (PECKOLS/PATOLS), thunder and fire god PERKŪNAS (PERCUN), and god of the sea and harvest POTRIMPO (PATRIMPAS).

THE SLAVIC TRIBES
the many faces of burnt sacrifices

The Slavs are the largest ethnolinguistic group in Europe, and were initially closely related to the proto-Balts. The 6th century Byzantine historian Procopius of Casesarea, described them:

> *"Since ancient times they have lived in the people's rule (democracy)... They believe that one of the gods, the creator of lightning, is the lord over all, and bulls are sacrificed to him and other sacred rites are performed. ... They worship rivers, and nymphs, and all sorts of other deities, and offer sacrifices to all of them."*

Another ancient source, the 1113 *Tale of Bygone Years* relates:

> *And Vladimir began to reign alone in Kiev. And he placed idols on the hill outside the palace: a Perun in wood with a silver head and a gold moustache, and Khors, Dazhdbog and Stribog and Simargl and Mokosh. And they offered sacrifices.*

The Slavs saw the cosmos as three-tiered: heaven at the top, represented by birds, the sun and the moon; earth in the middle, shown as bees and men; and an underworld at the bottom, symbolized by snakes and beavers, all ruled by the three-headed god Veles.

Many Slavic gods were carved in wood or stone, with three or four heads, and kept in temples on raised platforms, on hills or where two rivers met. Only the priests were allowed close access to them.

ABOVE: LEFT: *Procession of an idol of the god* VELES. *Processions of idols is a common feature of many polytheistic religions.* Right: *The gods* RUGYVITH, PREVITH, PORENUTH *and* SVANTOVIT. BELOW: *Idols, painting of enclosed temple by Nicholas Roerich, 1901.*

SLAVIC MYTHOLOGY
magic and mysticism

Slavic paganism evolved from an early worship of primordial forces, ancestors and a supreme being into a more complex mythology. The creator god was white-bearded ROD (or SUD). Lonely, he created LADA, goddess of love, and mother of Earth and all beings. He fashioned a golden egg, and placed it in the center of the waters, where it hatched SWAROG, god of fire, who then fashioned the rest of the world.

First among the next generation of gods was PERUN, god of thunder, law and war, who carried a mallet (like Perkūnas or Thor). DAZHBOGA was god of the Sun and of harvest, wealth and prosperity. MOKOSH was goddess of the earth, weaving and women's crafts, fertility and childbirth (along with the sisters ROZHANITSY). CHERNOBOG was god of darkness, death, and destruction.

MARZANNA was goddess of witchcraft, death and winter.

Perun's opposition was VELES, horned god of nature, magic, and the underworld. Their shrines were kept apart: Perun's on hilltops, and Veles' in the valleys and lowlands.

Veles is famous for his meeting with BABA YAGA, a clever hag living in a hut in the woods who could also take the form of a beautiful young woman (*right, by Jan Pienkowski*). Impressed, he made her the first shaman.

ABOVE: LEFT: The trickster god Veles, rival of Perun, shown as a wolf. CENTRE: Figurine of Perun from Veliky Novgorod, 12th C. RIGHT: The four sides of the 9th C. Zbruch Idol, Ukraine. Almost 9 feet tall, it may represent the unity of the three worlds and various gods.

ABOVE: Symbols for the gods are widely used: LEFT TO RIGHT: Hands of **SVAROG** (god); **KOLOVRAT**, the Sun; **VELES**, god of earth, water, livestock and the underworld.

LEFT: Adoration of the god **SVETOVID**, by Ivan Yakovlevich Bilibin, 1934, showing how the four faces were arranged around a pillar.

THE NORSE
away on expedition

The Nordic peoples inhabited what is now Denmark, Sweden and Norway. They spoke Old Norse, derived from Germanic Indo-European roots, and seem to have intermarried with the Sámi, who loaned them their boat designs, craftsmanship skills and religion, including the shamanic henbane potion of their Berserker warriors.

The old Norse word *viking* is an activity (to go viking); a *víkingr* was someone who went on sea expeditions. The 'Viking Age' began in 793, when the Norwegians and Danes attacked Lindisfarne monastery in England, and ended with the death of the last Norse king, Harold Hardrada, at the Battle of Stamford Bridge in 1066. By then the Vikings had built settlements in Greenland, Iceland, the Faroe Isles, Shetland, Orkney, the Outer Hebrides, northern Scotland, southwest Ireland, southern and eastern England, Normandy, southern Italy, Sicily, Tunisia and modern day Belarus (*see the Skalholt map, below*).

Much of what we know about Norse mythology comes from two books: the *Prose Edda*, written by Icelandic historian and lawspeaker Snorri Sturluson in 1223 (*see frontispiece*), and the *Poetic Edda*, a collection of 31 poems dating from the same time. The Nordic gods themselves may date back 1000 years or earlier, their origins lost in the mists of time.

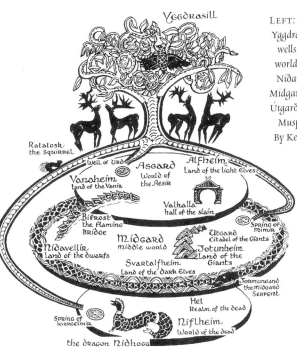

Yggdrasill

Ratatosk
the squirrel

Well of Urd

Asgard
World of
the Aesir

Alfheim
land of the light Elves

Vanaheim
land of the Vanir

Valhalla
hall of the slain

Bifrost
the flaming
bridge

Midgard
middle world

Utgard
Citadel of the Giants

Spring of
Mimir

Nidavellir
land of the dwarfs

Jotunheim
land of the
Giants

Svartalfheim
land of the dark Elves

Jormungand
the Midgard
serpent

Hel
Realm of the dead

Spring of
Hvergelmir

Niflheim
World of the dead

the dragon Nidhogg

LEFT: The Norse World Tree,
Yggdrasill, drinks from three
wells, and unifies the nine
worlds of Asgard, Álfheim,
Niðavellir / Svartálfaheim,
Midgard (Earth), Jötunheim /
Útgarð, Vanaheim, Niflheim,
Muspelheim (Fire) & Hel.
By Kevin Crossley-Holland.

FACING PAGE:
The Skalholt
map, showing the
Vikings' range. 17th
century version,
after Sigurður
Stefánsson's 16th
C. original. Iceland
is central; Norway
and Sweden on the
right; Greenland
arcs over the top.

V:14   Odin   VÖLVEN

LEFT: Odin and the Völva.
Völvas were female Norse
shamans who practiced
magic, known as Seidr (in
old Norse seiðr), meaning "to
bind". They wore colourful
dresses, gloves and a hat made
from cat fur. They also carried
a decorated staff or wand. In
the poem Völuspá, a Völva
warns Odin about Ragnarok,
the final demise of the gods.

NORDIC MYTHOLOGY
the birth of the gods

The world began in the yawning abyss of GINNUNGAGAP, between the realm of fire, MUSPELHEIM, and the realm of ice, NIFLHEIM. Here, as flames and ice met, the hissing steam formed the hermaphrodite frost giant YMIR ("Screamer"). Another version tells of a primordial goddess giant JORD who fell from the sky into the water to birth Ymir.

Ymir was fed by the primordial cow AUÐUMBLA, who licked salt off the ice and uncovered BÚRI, first of the AESIR gods. Búri's son BORR married BESTLA, daughter of the giant BOLTHORN. Their half-god half-giant children were ODIN and his brothers VILI and VE. Together, these slew Ymir and used their body to create the world. Flesh became earth, bones formed mountains, blood turned into rivers and lakes, and Ymir's skull formed the sky, with sparks of the original fire and ice becoming the stars and the moon.

Odin became ruler of the gods and lord of war, magic, wisdom and poetry. Obsessed with magic, he sacrificed an eye so he could drink from a magic well; he stabbed himself and hung himself from a tree for nine days and nights to learn the magic of the runes (*right*). He is often depicted with two ravens, HUGINN and MUNINN, riding his eight-legged horse SLEIPNIR.

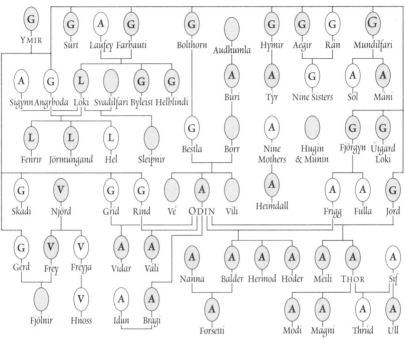

The family tree diagram contains the following entries:

Row 1: YMIR (G), Surt (G), Laufey (A), Farbauti (G), Bolthorn (G), Audhumla, Hymir (G), Aegir (G), Ran (G), Mundilfari (G)

Row 2: Sigynn (A), Angrboda (G), Loki (L), Svadilfari (G), Byleist (G), Helblindi, Buri (A), Tyr (A), Nine Sisters (G), Sol (A), Mani (A)

Row 3: Fenrir (L), Jörmungand (L), Hel (L), Sleipnir, Bestla (G), Borr (A), Nine Mothers, Hugin & Munin, Fjörgyn (G), Útgard Loki (G)

Row 4: Skadi (G), Njörd (V), Grid (G), Rind (G), Vé (A), ODIN (A), Vili, Heimdall (A), Frigg (A), Fulla (A), Jord (G)

Row 5: Gerd (G), Frey (V), Freyja (V), Vidar (A), Vali (A), Nanna (A), Balder (A), Hermod (A), Hoder (A), Meili (A), THOR (A), Sif (A)

Row 6: Fjölnir (V), Hnoss (V), Idun (A), Bragi (A), Forseti (A), Modi (A), Magni (A), Thrúd (A), Ull (A)

ABOVE: The Norse gods' family tree is an intricate web of divine relationships. At its core lies a mighty progenitor, whose offspring include gods of thunder, wisdom, mischief, and war. Amidst intermarriages and complex connections, these deities form a divine tapestry the shape of which varies depending on the source material.

G - Giant
− - Giant's line
A - Aesir Gods
V - Vanir Gods
L - Loki family
◯ - Female
◯ - Male/other

LEFT: One-eyed Odin ("Óðinn", Old Norse) riding his horse Sleipnir, from Ólafur Brynjúlfsson's 1760s edition of Snorri Sturluson 13th century Prose Edda.

THE NORSE PANTHEON
gods and goddesses

Odin fathered many children. With the goddess Jord he produced **THOR**, god of thunder, lightning and storms. Thor carried a mighty hammer **MJOLNIR** and rode a chariot pulled by two goats, **TANNGRISNIR** (tooth grinder) and **TANNGNJÓSTR** (tooth gnasher). He was married to **SIF**, goddess of agriculture, producing sons **MAGNI** and **MODI**. But it was **FRIGG**, goddess of marriage, motherhood and prophecy, who Odin loved most. Together they produced **BALDR**, god of light and purity; **HODR**, blind god of winter and darkness, who was tricked by Loki into killing Baldr; **HERMOD**, the messenger god of swiftness; **HNOSS**, goddess of beauty and precious things; **GERSEMI**, goddess of fertility and abundance.

Odin also had children with various giantesses: **TYR**, god of war and justice, with **HYMIR**; **VALI**, god of vengeance with **RINDR**; **VIDAR**, god of silence, with **GRID**; **BRAGI**, god of poetry, with **GUNNLOD**; and **HEIMDALL**, god of light and vengeance, with nine giantesses.

Then there was **FREYJA**, goddess of love, fertility, war and magic, daughter of Vanir sea god **NJORD** and his sister **NERTHUS** (**SKADI**).

And **LOKI**, son of giants, the smooth-talking, shape-shifting, sex-changing trickster god of fire and air, who stole Thor's hammer.

ODIN, *with ravens & wolves*

FRIGG, *with* FULLA.

THOR, *with hammer & goats*

FREYJA, *with her big cats*

HILDISVINI, *Freyja's attendant*

the giantess HYROKKIN

ABOVE: FRIGGA *spinning the clouds*, John Dollman, 1909. LEFT: *The goddess* FREYJA *abducted by the giants* FASOLT *and* FAFNER, Arthur Rackham, 1910. "Friday" is named after Freyja, "Freyja's day", associating her with the planet Venus. FACING PAGE: LOKI *tricks* IDUN, *goddess of youth and immortality*, John Bauer, 1911.

GODS & GODDESSES

GOD(DESS)	SAMI	FINNIC	BALTIC	SLAVIC	NORDIC
EARTH/MOTHER	Máttatáhkká	Akka	Zemyna	Mat Zemlya	Jörd
SUN	Beaivi	Paivatar	Saule	Svarog	Sol
MOON	Mánnu	Kuu	Meness	Khors	Mani
SKY	Radien	Taara	Dievs	Triglav	Tyr
THUNDER	Horagalles	Ukko	Perkūnas	Perun	Thor
SEA	Ahti	Ahti	Bangpūtys	Veles	Rán
WAR	-	Tursas	Junda	Svetovid	Valkyries
FERTILITY/BIRTH	Akka	Akras	Laima	Jarovit	Frigg
HARVEST	-	Pekko	Javine	Jarovit	Freyja
DEATH	Jábmiidáhkká	Kalma	Mara	Morana	Hel
HUNT	Juksáhkká	Mielikki	Medžiojma	Devana	Ullr
WIND	Bieggolmai	Tuuletar	Vejopatis	Striborg	Njörd
LOVE/MAGIC	Gieddegeažegálgu	Lempo	Milda	Ziva	Freyja

FEASTS AND FESTIVALS

North European pagans measured time using nature as a guide: moon and sun phases, animal migrations, crop seasons. Norse hunter-gatherers divided the year into hunting and breeding seasons. The Sámi had eight seasons based on reindeer cycles. Equinoxes and solstices were celebrated markers. As with the names of gods and goddesses, similar festivals varied in name across tribes and locations. Dates also varied.

JANUARY - Žvaigždžių diena (Baltic) - The Day of stars. Oddajagemánnu (Sami) - New Year.

FEBRUARY - Dísablót (Norse) - Fertility Festival. Þorrablót (Norse) - Thor's Festival.

MARCH - Pavasario Lygė (Baltic), Njukčamánnu (Sami) - Spring Equinox.

APRIL - Jorė (Baltic) - Spring Festival. Cuoŋománnu (Sami) - Snow Crust Month.

MAY - Sigrblót (Norse) - Freya/Summer festival. Miessemánnu (Sami) Reindeer Calf Month.

JUNE - Midsummarblót (Norse) - Summer Solstice. Semik (Slavic) - Festival of the Dead.

JULY - Rugių šventė (Baltic) - Rye Festival. Suiodnemánnu (Sami) - Hay Month.

AUGUST - Perkūnas Day (Baltic) - Hay Harvest Festival. Borgemánnu (Sami) - Molt Month.

SEPTEMBER - Rudens Lygė (Baltic) - Autumnal Equinox. Čakčamánnu (Sami) - Fall Month.

OCTOBER - Golggotmánnu (Sami) - Rut Month. Alfarblót (Norse) Harvest/Winter.

NOVEMBER - Ilgės (Baltic) - All Soul's Day. Skábmamánnu (Sami) - Dark Period Month.

DECEMBER - Žiemos saulėgrįža (Baltic) - Winter Solstice. Jól or Yule (various) - Odin/Wild Hunt.